MESSAGE

FROM THE

MOON

An inspirational and spiritually uplifting guide
for living a full and satisfied life!

CAROL WALKER–RUSSELL, J.D.

MESSAGE FROM THE MOON
By Carol Walker-Russell, J.D.

Scriptures marked KJV are taken from the KING JAMES VERSION (KJV): KING JAMES VERSION, public domain.

Trade paperback ISBN:978-0-5787714-0-3

"I will bless the Lord at all times: his praise shall continually be in my mouth. My soul shall make her boast in the Lord: the humble shall hear thereof, and be glad. O magnify the Lord with me, and let us exalt his name together."

Psalms 34:1-3 (King James Version)

DEDICATIONS

Marie Walker

Sunrise: Wednesday, July 20, 1927
Sunset: Sunday, May 30, 2010

I had the extreme honor and privilege of being birthed and raised by Marie Walker, a truly phenomenal woman. Mama (as I call her, and if you didn't have a mother like Mama, please feel free to call her Mama as well) was the funniest, smartest, strongest woman that I have ever known. Although Mama never had the opportunity to complete high school, attend college, or obtain a degree from an institution of higher learning, she could run circles around most that did. Her strength and honor were rooted and grounded in her profound faith in God and belief in His love that can, and indeed will, overcome anything. This book is proudly dedicated to the memory of my mother, Marie Walker, who gave everything so that her children could achieve anything!

Greg Russell, Sr.

To my wonderful husband and best friend, Greg Russell, I proudly dedicate this book. In 1983, we met playing the "Pac Man" video game. Although you still will not admit that I beat you, I thank God every day for our amazing journey through life together. On September 3, 2020, we were blessed to celebrate 32 wonderful years of marriage. You still captivate my heart with your kindness, warmth, gentle spirit, yet boldness that surrounds me like a shield of protection. Thank you for your love, devotion and dedication to me, our son, and family through the years. You are a wonderful husband, father, and person of unwavering faith. I am incredibly blessed and simply could not have completed this book without your abiding love and support.

Gregory Russell, Jr.

To our son, Gregory Russell, Jr., I dedicate this book. Before you were formed in my womb, I was told by several doctors that I could never have children. Well, the doctors were obviously wrong! Your birth ushered a burst of light into our lives as a constant reminder of God's amazing power, grace, and how faith always trumps fear. Thank you for being the blessing that you are. It is a privilege to have been chosen by God to serve as your mother. I always strived to be an inspiration to you and wrote the poem "Reach for the Stars Son" for your high school graduation in 2014. God has blessed me with many gifts, son, but you are my treasure and greatest miracle!

TABLE OF CONTENTS

INTRODUCTION

"If any man be in Christ, he is a new creature: old things are passed away; behold, all things are become new."
2 Corinthians 5:17 (King James Version)

I'm sure that by now you're wondering, just who is Carol Walker-Russell? Well, please take a seat and allow me to introduce myself. Currently, I serve as a Judge with the Office of State Administrative Hearings, where I have had the pleasure of successfully resolving disputes between the public and state agencies since August 16, 2000. My extensive work history includes experiences as a private practitioner, in which I handled civil litigation as well as criminal defense of felony and misdemeanor prosecutions; Adjunct Law Professor of Litigation; State Court Chief Assistant Solicitor

General, in which I tried hundreds of misdemeanor cases and managed the office staff; Law Clerk to a State Court Judge, in which I researched and wrote orders on a variety of complex litigation matters; Certified Mediator, in which I assisted parties in resolving disputes without litigation; Magistrate Court Judge, and Recorder's Court (Traffic) Judge. Throughout my career, I remained highly dedicated and devoted to community service and recognize the need to reach back to help others.

I have been writing poetry since I was a child, but never shared my writings. Although still protective and a little guarded, I promise to be as transparent as possible and think that you will find my story to be actually quite interesting. I was raised by a single mother, Marie Walker, as her seventh child of eight. Yes, I am that strangely unusual, yet oddly gifted seventh child. Unfortunately, my father died when I was age two, so I have no memory of him. However, I have never felt fatherless. Even as a child, I always knew the presence of my Heavenly Father and that He constantly surrounded, protected, and watched over me. No, I didn't just "feel" God's presence; I "knew" it and understood the difference. Stay tuned for details later in the book. For now, you need a little more about my story.

When I was around age 8, Mama moved us to the Atlanta Bowen Homes Housing Projects. Even today, I vividly recall the beautiful landscape of the community that was filled with lush, green grass. Everything was kept so neat and clean. Back then, there were very high standards for residents. Lawns were kept neatly cut, window shades were mandatory white and strictly raised to a certain height and as Mama's children we were, of course, very well-mannered. Mama was a strict disciplinarian and for that I am eternally grateful. All of Mama's children graduated high school and none went to prison. I just heard somebody say "Amen!"

Contrary to popular belief, life for us in the "Projects" was actually quite good. In fact, I didn't know that we were "poor" until somebody told me. I still disagree. We were never without food, clothing, shelter, toys, imagination, good neighbors, and most importantly God's overwhelming joy! Although we did not have much money, we were rich! Even as a child, I was a "book worm" who constantly read and graduated as the "Best All Around" student from A.D. Williams Elementary School. I then attended Frederick Douglas High School, where I graduated with honors. After high school, I obtained my Bachelor of Science degree in

Criminal Justice from Georgia State University (1983) and Juris Doctorate from Georgia State University, College of Law (1987).

As a young child, I quickly discovered that I had a unique gift of writing. Well, actually, the "gift" found me. I was a quiet, shy child and kept mostly to myself. In those quiet moments, I began writing daily inspirational messages to myself and would often share them with others. I would write on my hands, calendars, scratch paper, book covers, even toilet tissue, just to get the words out. I had no idea of what God had planted inside me, just waiting to burst out. In 1973, I wrote my first poem, "Joy," at age 12, which still warms my heart and spirit. I have been writing ever since, but slowed by the interruptions of life such as college, law school, marriage, the birth of our son, work as a law clerk, Prosecutor, Defense Attorney, owner of my own law firm, Mediator, adjunct Law Professor, Recorder's Court/Traffic Court Judge, Magistrate Court Judge, and an Administrative Law Judge for 20 years. Although still busy, I am now ready to share with you the beautiful words that have constantly poured into me by the Creator of the Universe.

Enclosed you will find poems written from my heart to inspire, "Bench Notes" to offer words of wisdom from the perspective of a seasoned jurist, and follow-up dialogues to discuss my interpretation of my writings and what God's words say about a given situation. Finally, just in case you're wondering, yes there really is a "MESSAGE FROM THE MOON." This poem was written on a train ride back to London from Paris in September 2018 while celebrating our 30th wedding anniversary and is truly captivating, even to me! It literally takes my breath away to imagine that the moon hasn't just shined on the earth since creation, but actually witnessed every moment of time and delivered its own message for mankind. So, which poem or Bench Note will be your favorite? Just keep turning the page. Of course, I saved some of the best for last.

Blessings!

Carol Walker-Russell

"JOY"

My joy is pure and simple
It can be neither bought, nor sold
It's worth much more than silver
And its value outweighs gold

It shines a golden image
On my face, which does display
The joy I feel within my heart and
Soul from day to day

I know that joy is very rare
You have to pay the price
But for joy, you don't spend a dime
Just believe in Jesus Christ!

"Thou wilt shew me the path of life: in thy presence is fullness of joy; at thy right hand there are pleasures for evermore."

Psalms 16:11 (King James Version)

"JOY"
Inspirational Dialogue

Oh, the wonders of pure "Joy" as seen through the innocent eyes of a child. Even at age 12, I knew that real joy reaches the soul from within. I have been joyful my entire life and it is ironic that my name, "Carol" actually means "joyous song, or song of joy." Joy is a gifted measure of delight that swells to warm the heart and spirit. Joy is indeed priceless! You can't buy it, sell it, or barter for it. Many have tried and failed.

Joy begins with the understanding that you have a divine purpose in life and are never left alone to achieve it. With joy, you smile when there's no one else in the room. Your heart sings a melody when there is no music to be heard and your spirit feels the presence of a power so great, words are just inadequate. You feel joy by choice and on purpose. However, you must be open to receiving joy.

Even in your darkest hour, you can feel joy because you are eternally connected to its main power source. The easiest way to overcome thoughts of despair is to meditate on the goodness and greatness of God and tap into the natural melody of song that God placed in your heart before you were formed in your mother's womb. Trust me, joy is in there! Whenever you're feeling a little "down," awaken your joyful spirit with a quick "pick me up" by listening to some good praise music. I guarantee that it works every time. Remember, when praises go up, "Joy" comes down!

"GREETINGS FROM GOD"

Greetings from God from whom all ages past

Who made the valleys deep and the mountains last

From God who calmed the stormy sea

The first, the last, our eternity

Greetings from our Lord

Who stands on Heaven's high

But hears His children's faintest cry

"Lord thou hast been our dwelling place in all generations. Before the mountains were brought forth, or ever thou hadst formed the earth and the world, even from everlasting to everlasting, thou art God."

Psalms 90:1-2 (King James Version)

"GREETINGS FROM GOD"
Inspirational Dialogue

Although I was only 12 when I penned this poem, I clearly understood the awesome magnificence of our God's power and the wonders of His majesty. Even now, I often recite this short poem to acknowledge God's everlasting creations and His omnipotence. The recognition that the most powerful Creator of the entire Universe knows us individually and cares about our deepest concerns is comforting to the soul.

God sends His greetings to us each day in the beauty, majesty and calmness of the morning sunrise, the twinkling of the moonlight in the starry sky, the healing coolness of the ocean breeze, the beautiful melodious pitch of the songbirds, and the glory of the iridescent rainbow. His greetings are bountiful and endless. You don't have to look too far, or spend a dime, to see God's wondrous greetings. They are all around us. All you have to do is open your eyes to receive them.

"DONE DID IT NOW"
(Written in Negro Dialect)

Ain't no use in sheddin' tears
Cryin' 'bout that race un-won
Get up off that lazy rocker
'Preciate the thangs that's done

No use sittin' in that corner
Lights all off and tears a flowin'
You done did it now, ya hear?
Stop those tears and start a goin'

Time is out for pity pettin'
Time to straighten out this mess
You just think about 'yo tryin'
You done gave 'yo very best

Ain't I learned you to keep on tryin'?
Ain't I learned you when and how?
Don't you sit down in that corner
Cause honey, you done did it now!

"If we confess our sins, he is faithful and just to forgive us our sins, and to cleanse us from all unrighteousness."
1 John 1:9 (King James Version)

"DONE DID IT NOW"
Inspirational Dialogue

I will never forget the day that I wrote "Done Did it Now." I was age sixteen and experiencing the normal frustrations of being a teenager. I recall feelings of awkwardness and just wanting to fit in. Late in the quietness of a hot summer evening, I was in my bedroom and felt the presence and spirit of a female ancestor (whom I have never met or seen) appear to calm and comfort me. She clearly knew me and spoke in a language that I can only describe as "negro dialect."

After our conversation, I immediately wrote this poem to capture the memory of our conversation. I wrote this poem in the language that she spoke, which I clearly understood. When I read "Done Did it Now" to Mama, she laughed and laughed. I knew then that I had captured the true meaning of my late ancestor's message and have carried it in my heart to comfort me through many years of trials and tribulations. Trust me, I have had many!

This poem captures the true essence of reflection, self-forgiveness, and the need to shake off the spirit of self-pity in order to grow up and move forward. The poem's simple, yet powerful message of letting go of the past resonates deep within the spirit. From this poem, I learned long ago to do this one important thing: forget those things which are behind, and instead reach forward unto those things which lie ahead (Philippians 3:13).

"IN SEARCH OF PEACE"

This mean old world is setting out

to make life's journey rougher

Man's wicked works and evil spirit only makes a

difficult battle tougher

To find some comfort in this world

is not beyond all reach

Yet, no man who could ever speak, sing,

pray, or preach

Has found the great solution

that the universe so needs

In order to find happiness beyond its evil deeds

Instead of searching out the peace

that's nowhere to be found

We're reaching for false hopes and dreams and

standing on loose grounds

Of all man's accomplishments
and all that he's discovered
Earth's serenity is buried deep
and yet to be uncovered

Man is content that he has spent millions
in outer space
But very little can he afford
on things he can't replace

He'll sell his soul for silver and gold
and metals that will rust
Not realizing that he too will fade
and return to ash and dust

Oh, if only man could understand the triviality
of man-made things and
See God's beauty shining bright through
rivers and through streams

The peacefulness of sunny days,
the singing birds in trees
The morning glories sparkling
and the humming of the bees

The crisp, cool air in autumn
and how mellow is the rain
That dampens the earth's green surface from hill to
valley, plain to plain

No diamond, pearl, or ruby can instill into a soul
The immortality of God's wonders
that's a blessing to behold

The only thing that's missing on this earth
that's Godly lighted
Is man's love for one another,
which stands yet to be ignited

A little love and understanding,
mixed with reason and some cheer
Could bring peace a little closer
and serenity a little near

If we'd dampen the earth's dry surface

with a drop or two of care

We could see beyond our foggy ways and know

we're almost there

But our efforts in this battle

that all men must take part

Would be in vain if we're not careful and plan all

actions from the heart

In the end, we'd all float upward to a place of

triumphant bliss

Glancing down, without regrets,

we'd see no unsaved soul was missed

"The Lord will give strength unto his people; the Lord will bless his people with peace."

Psalms 29:11 (King James Version)

"IN SEARCH OF PEACE"
Inspirational Dialogue

At age 19, this poem was a confirmation to me that I was blessed and endowed with the gift of writing poetry and remains one of my favorites. It still gives me chills! I truly believe that it was divinely inspired and literally poured into me by God. I wrote this poem while riding the public transportation bus to and from college during my freshman year. I vividly remember having my first sudden urgency to write and began jotting the words on scraps of paper that I found in my book bag.

From the beginning, I knew that this poem would be special and different from the others because of its intense depth and meaningful universal message. So, I continued to gather scraps of paper and wrote until satisfied that it was completed. Even now, when I read "In Search of Peace," it moves my spirit and reaches my core.

It leaves a powerful reminder that we owe each other the responsibility to seek a civilized, unified, humanitarian, and peaceful coexistence. God has already bestowed within us the ability to transform this world into a perfect place of peace. All required is that we follow His lead, reach within ourselves to transform, and love one another (John 15:17).

"REACH FOR THE STARS SON"

When life throws a curve ball to darken your path
Your way seems uncertain, unclear
Just reach for the stars son to brighten your road
Although distant, a star's reach is near

Stars brighten the darkest of nights
Although thousands of light years away
And just like your dreams,
When one star fades
Another star just takes its place

When you reach for the Stars son,
You never give up
No matter how hard your way seems
You stay in the game and fight the good fight
To reach those impossible dreams

See, life is a journey that's never complete
Without rainfall along the way
But after the storm, the sun always shines
To brighten the darkest day

So, reach for the stars son in all that you do
Never give up or give in!
For quitting's no option for those who believe
That their star will shine bright in the end

"I can do all things through Christ which strengtheneth me."
Philippians 4:13 (King James Version)

"REACH FOR THE STARS SON"
Inspirational Dialogue

I wrote this poem for our son, Gregory, Jr., on his 18th birthday. Throughout his life, we have encouraged Gregory to pursue his dreams and become all that God created him to be. I still constantly remind Gregory that he is God's chosen warrior and a champion for truth and justice. As we were talking on his 18th birthday, I stopped mid-sentence and told Gregory, "I'll be right back," because I had this familiar and overwhelming urge to write.

Within fifteen minutes, I returned with the poem "Reach For The Stars Son" in hand. Gregory was amazed that I could write an entire poem so quickly, but I was not. I realized long ago that the gifts and talents that God pours into us flow down quickly, as a mighty stream, when they are called into action.

Through many years, I have continued to encourage anyone in need of uplifting to "reach for the stars" and not become complacent or weary in well doing. For in due season, you will reap, if you faint not (Galatians 6:9). Now, Gregory has this poem written just for him to prove it!

"BE A RAINMAKER"
Bench Note

Each of us comes here with seeds of greatness stored inside. Whether those seeds ever take root and flourish depends upon the degree of nourishment they receive. In order to take root, seeds are planted into the dark earth where there is no light. Amazingly, over time and with careful watering, the seed breaks out of its shell and transforms into a flowering plant that climbs out of the darkness into the light. Similarly, the seeds of greatness buried deep inside of us also need watering and will only germinate after being showered with inspiration, confidence, motivation, support, hope, and encouragement.

Whether we ever become all that we were meant to be depends upon the amount of rain that we receive from each other. Each one of us can be a rainmaker. Not the kind of rainmaker that brings in new business and wins new accounts almost magically, but a rainmaker who brings people to self-awareness and motivates mystically. The true essence of being a great rainmaker is not measured in the abundance of what you bring but by the magnitude of what you have left behind. Undoubtedly, after such down pouring of rain, we give each other substances necessary for growth to bring forth our unique talents and fruits in abundance.

Let it rain…Let it rain!

"Though I speak with the tongues of men and of angels, and have not charity, I am become as sounding brass, or a tinkling cymbal. And though I have the gift of prophecy, and understand all mysteries, and all knowledge; and though I have all faith, so that I could remove mountains, and have not charity, I am nothing… And now abideth faith, hope, charity, these three; but the greatest of these is charity."

1 Corinthians 13: 1-2, 13 (King James Version)

"BE A RAINMAKER"
Inspirational Dialogue

"Be a Rainmaker" was written in 2015 as my first message to the Gate City Bar Association when I served as the Judicial Section Chair. The simple, yet powerful message is that the true essence of a great rainmaker knows no boundaries and begins with an immeasurable benevolence towards others and those less fortunate than ourselves. There is no greater act of charity than seeing a need of another and making a conscious effort to fulfill it.

Each of us requires help from another at some time in our life. We all desire to feel loved, respected, encouraged, mentored and acknowledged, which can only come from outside of ourselves. A kind and compassioned heart, words of hope with encouragement, and doing good works towards others pour down like rain as powerful nourishment to lift dejected spirits with feelings of hopelessness, inadequacies and despair.

Charity shows itself with compassionate good works towards others. Otherwise, it is meaningless and no charity at all. Words alone are simply insufficient because real charity requires action. Like faith, charity if it does not have works is dead (James 2:17)!

"YOUR GIFTS WILL FIND YOU!"
Bench Note

Every Friday he would come home drunk with a bunch of collard greens and a can of salmon. My late mother always laughed uncontrollably when she told me this story of her friend's husband who roamed the streets all week but managed to drag home each Friday to feed his wife and small children. Whenever her friend complained about the "groceries" that he brought home, her husband would routinely storm out of the house and she wouldn't see him again until the next Friday. Of course, he returned again with, you guessed it, a bunch of collard greens and a can of salmon. This cycle continued for years until Mom's friend got sick of her husband, the greens and salmon. So, she left him with children in tow.

She was fortunate to find an attorney willing to take her case pro bono. The attorney not only gave her free legal advice but reminded her that she deserved a life far better than the one that she had been willing to accept. When she heard the attorney's words, something leaped inside of her. For the first time, she heard words of encouragement that inspired her to move forward on her new journey as a single parent, which was scary. At first, she didn't think that she had any talents until she got a job as a seamstress and discovered her true gifts. Not only could she sew but created such beautifully tailored clothes that she was able to open her own business, buy her own home, and provide for herself and children. My mother's laugh still echoes the absurd actions of her friend's ex-husband. Yet, it was his callous treatment that catapulted her friend to find her inner strength, passion, and true purpose.

Such as it is in life. We are often driven to greatness by refusing to settle for the meager crumbs that others offer. Deep inside, we all know that we deserve better and so much more. When we settle for less, we not only deprive ourselves of a meaningful and purpose driven life, but we rob our conscience of the ability to reach its full potential. Ironically, the very actions that endeavor to hold us down can actually propel us into our true destiny. We all have negative things that happen to us. Some are more unbearable than others. However, after every experience you gain knowledge, power, and a greater understanding. Nothing in life is ever wasted. Not even a bunch of greens or a can of salmon.

"So we, being many, are one body in Christ, and every one members one of another. Having then gifts differing according to the grace that is given to us."

Romans 12: 5-6 (King James Version)

"YOUR GIFTS WILL FIND YOU!"
Inspirational Dialogue

"Your Gifts Will Find You" was written as my second message to the Gate City Bar Association when I served as the Judicial Section Chair. The magnificent essence of its meaning is that each of us is endowed with unique gifts and talents that were planted inside by the Creator of the Universe before we were even formed in our mother's womb (Jeremiah 1:5, KJV). We all have different gifts according to the grace given by God to help complete our designated assignments. Our challenge is tilling the soul to break free from the strongholds that bind. Only then can we access the abundant seeds that are buried deep, yet waiting to break forth, and awaken those hidden treasures that compel us to rise and meet our divine purpose.

One of the most difficult tasks is the recognition that our most painful trials and tribulations are often used as the best tillers to awaken those hidden talents buried deep within. We know that "all things work together for the good of them that love God, to them who are the called according to His purpose" (Romans 8:28, KJV). However, many lack a clear understanding of what this well-known scripture actually means.

As a loving child of God, everything that happens to you is not only known by God, but orchestrated to be used for your benefit with an ultimate good outcome. Although it may not seem to be good while you are going through it, each circumstance fits perfectly into your unique "puzzle" that God created and specially designed to help develop your special gifts and enable you to grow into the unique person that you were created to be. Everything in life serves a divine purpose and absolutely nothing is ever wasted!

"CALLING ALL GLADIATORS!"
Bench Note

"Law and Order," that's how my brother introduces me to his friends. I can't help but smile each time I hear him say it. I'm "seven of eight" in my lineage of siblings and I was the only one fortunate to be able to go to college and law school. I vividly remember that first day of law school. The Contracts Professor told our class to "look to the left and to the right." He then said, "One of you won't be back next year." You and I were the lucky ones. We survived that first year and not only graduated from law school but passed the bar exam to become licensed Attorneys at Law.

Now, do you remember why you went to law school? Think for a moment. Go down memory lane to a slower, simpler place in time. Ah yes, there it is. Now you remember. You were all fired up and ready to change the world as a champion of truth and justice! You would fight the good fight and let nothing stand in your way. In other words, you wanted to be a modern-day Gladiator.

Ancient roman Gladiators were known for their strength and courage. They were armed combatants who either survived the fight or died valiantly in the arena. Modern-day Gladiators are no less courageous. Indeed, the issues of today call for such champion fighters who understand that one person really can make an overwhelming difference in the world and other people lives.

Gladiators understand that they are a committee of one and don't need a champion to get things done. They volunteer their time selflessly to those less fortunate and stand in formation for the call of duty to serve. Gladiators give hope to the hopeless; strength to the weak; help feed the hungry and clothe the naked; give a listening ear to those in need; provide a shoulder to lean on for the weary; and give exceptional legal services in every case.

The truth is, every attorney is a Gladiator (or as my brother prefers to call us, "Law and Order"). It is no coincidence that we survived law school. We have been bestowed unique knowledge and capabilities that few people have been chosen to possess. The fire that ignited our passion to withstand the rigors of law school still smolders inside of us. Awaken the passion and fan that flame. Now, grab your shield and serve!

"He hath shewed thee, O man, what is good; and what doth the Lord require of thee, but to do justly, and to love mercy, and to walk humbly with thy God?"

Micah 6:8 (King James Version)

"CALLING ALL GLADIATORS!"
Inspirational Dialogue

"Calling All Gladiators" was written in 2015 as my third message to the Gate City Bar Association, when I served as the Judicial Section Chair to inspire attorneys to rededicate themselves to their true purpose and passion as legally trained "Gladiators." Undoubtedly, attorneys serve our society well as important warriors in the legal arena. However, every loving child of God is also a designated soldier or Gladiator, and is armed with strength for every battle.

As with attorneys, your true purpose as a Gladiator can only be fulfilled when you give hope to the hopeless; strength for the weak; feed the hungry, clothe the naked; give a listening ear to others in need; and provide a steady shoulder for the weary to lean on. You are already endowed by the Creator of the Universe and don't need a formal education, title, or committee approval to be God's Gladiator. All that's required is that you fully commit to "do justly, love mercy, and walk humbly with God." Now, grab *your* shield and serve!

"LIVE A LASTING LEGACY!"
Bench Note

I'm still in awe over the 1960s. Its reformative impact on society forever changed our laws and the course of our lives. When I think of their generation of brave, strong-willed foot soldiers, I can't help but to feel nostalgic. Dr. Martin Luther King, Jr.'s "I Have a Dream" speech was delivered in 1963 when I was but a child. Yet, I still vividly remember hearing the speech played as my mother did chores around the house and cooked dinner. Each time I heard that speech, I literally stopped playing with my toys and listened in total captivation.

Dr. King expressed a vision of a world where people from every race are united and judged not based on the color of their skin, but solely upon the content of their character. Those powerful words were branded into my conscience. Even as a child, I understood that our legacies are based upon the individual choices we make and the life that we choose to live.

Fast forward to 2015 and I am well into adulthood. Dr. King, my father, mother, and many of those great warriors have all passed away. Each time I hear of the death of a person in their generation, I truly feel that another star has faded, and the world has gotten a little darker. There's a solemn realization that the torch has now passed to *my* generation and I wonder if we are ready for the many challenges ahead. Are we willing to reach the high bar that has been set by those who have gone before us? Will we teach our children to value life and learning? Will *we* have a village of caring, compassionate neighbors who actually know each other's names?

We had the unique privilege of being taught life's lessons by a generation of powerful and unforgettable people who left a strong foundation from which to build a better and brighter world. We stand on their shoulders and owe it to their legacies, and our own, to reach our fullest potential. We *must* finish the tasks that they have left behind and willingly accept the torch that has been passed to us. In other words, remember the game that you played so happily when we were children? Well, "TAG, YOU'RE IT!"

"And I saw the dead, small and great, stand before God; and the books were opened: and another book was opened, which is *the book* of life: and the dead were judged out of those things which were written in the books, according to their works."

Revelations 20:12 (King James Version)

"LIVE A LASTING LEGACY!"
Inspirational Dialogue

"Live a Lasting Legacy!" was written in 2015 as my final message to the Gate City Bar Association, when I served as the Judicial Section Chair. Its enduring message is that the length of our lives is measured by God, uncertain, and short as a mist. For one day we are here, but very soon we're gone (James 4:14). We are all given a clean slate when we arrive out of our mother's womb. How we fill our slate depends upon the choices that we make during the course of our brief lives. Therefore, there must be recognition that we only have a finite number of earthly days to accomplish our designated assignments.

Still, we are encouraged that God gives us sufficient time to accomplish our assignments if we are not ignorant of this one thing, "that one day is with the Lord as a thousand years, and a thousand years as one day" (2 Peter 3:8). Each generation is tasked with the responsibility and obligation to accept the torch that has been passed and complete any unfinished works left behind by those who came before them. This is one of the greatest callings on our lives and cannot be abdicated or forgotten.

God often uses multiple generations to complete His divine purpose and we must remember that His thoughts and ways are not as ours (Isaiah 55:8). Our legacies are defined by our works here on earth. However, upon completing those works, we can rejoice in knowing that we are blessed when we die in the Lord, we will soon rest from our labors, and our works here on earth do follow us (Revelations 14:13).

"I HOPE YOU FAIL!"

May your dreams be filled with wonders
Too breathtaking to withhold
May your goals be met with **boldness**
Leaving nothing left untold

May you glance back on your journey
Of life's accomplishments along your trail
May you find the joy in knowing
Along the way that you must fail

I hope you fail so you will learn
That you cannot always win and
The battles that you fight the most
Are often from within

For in failure you gain courage and
The strength to overcome
To keep from fighting battles
That you've already won

Failure transforms fear to fearless

Weakness to power, tears to joy

For on the brink of failure

Determination will deploy

In failure you are humbled and

Then take a second glance

At all of those shortcomings

That you thought were brought by chance

Tears of failure water greatness

That is often buried deep

Shattered dreams are reawakened

To bring victory beyond belief

As you look upon your trophies and

Those plaques upon your wall

Yes, be proud of all your studies and

The lessons that you'll recall

But remember that it was failure
That brought you to your knees
To lift your hands towards heaven
In those desperate, heartfelt pleas

I hope you find life's true purpose
As you travel along the way
But my wish for you is greater
Than these words can ever say

For I send you my best wishes and
My prayer is you'll fare well
But glancing back upon your journey
Along the way, I hope you fail

"The steps of a good man are ordered by the Lord: and he delighteth in his way. Though he fall, he shall not be utterly cast down: for the Lord upholdeth him with his hand."
Psalms 37:23-24 (King James Version)

"I HOPE YOU FAIL!"
Inspirational Dialogue

There is no greater instructor for success in life than the inescapable gift of failure. At some point, we all must fail. As children, many were taught to believe that you must always win and take home a trophy. However, we are forced to learn that this concept is misguided and totally unrealistic. We grow and mature as true winners only when we meet and overcome our most difficult challenges. Otherwise, we are destined to remain complacent and stagnant.

Failure forces us to fight for our chosen destiny and refuse to settle for anything less. However, overcoming failure is not easy and often comes at a hefty price. Failure truly can "bring us to our knees to lift our hands towards heaven in desperate, heartfelt pleas." However, failure also humbles us to re-examine the misguided belief that our successes are due to our own strength, knowledge and capabilities, rather than being anointed gifts from God.

We were never created to find true satisfaction through winning every battle. For, that is far too shallow. Instead, it is more victorious to "trust in the Lord with all of your heart, lean not to your own understanding, and in all your ways, acknowledge him knowing that he shall direct your paths" (Proverbs 3:5-6). Only then, will you gain magnificent joy and understand that along this uncertain journey of life, you must fail.

"A CHRISTMAS GIFT"

It was weeks before Christmas,

I will always remember

The night I found Jesus in early December

The house was all decked out in lights all aglow

The streets were all covered in blankets of snow

There were presents all stacked

under a twinkling tree

The gifts were all wrapped for my family and me

The music that played filled the house full of cheer

Everybody celebrating that Christmas was near

As I stood at a window and gazed with a glance

There stood a tall deer about to give prance

But instead of him fleeing

when he saw our eyes meet

He slowly walked towards me in snow covered feet

Then he stopped at the sight

of our tree near the street

For under it stood a nativity

Three wise men stood guard with presents in hand

They had traveled afar from their distant homeland

For they'd heard that a messiah

had been sent from above

A gift for all ages, a treasure of love

Lying there in a manger for the whole world to see

A gift for all ages through eternity

The deer stood there captive

as he stared at the scene

Then did something strange

as he looked straight at me

This deer slowly bowed as he stood in the snow

For he knew this gift was sent

from Heaven to below

He stayed there bowed as I took in this sight
Then I felt something strange
on that cold winter's night
I felt love all forgiving and peace from all fears
Then I felt on my face the streaming of tears

For this deer got God's message
with fur covered feet
A message from Heaven as he passed on the street
I stayed there in wonder as the deer slowly stood
Amazed at this gift in my own neighborhood

I will never forget that wonderful sight
As I glanced out my window
that cold winter's night
For I knew what I witnessed was a sign from above
Of God's grace and mercy, and undying love

"For God so loved the world, that he gave his only begotten Son, that whosoever believeth in him should not perish, but have everlasting life."

John 3:16 (King James Version)

"A CHRISTMAS GIFT"
Inspirational Dialogue

The splendor of the Christmas season is a magically captivating reminder of God's eternal love for all of mankind. The beauty of Christmas with its breathtaking iridescent lights, decorated trees, vivid and colorful ornaments, music, decadent food, entertainment and incomparable joy flows from person to person in celebration of the birth of our Lord and Savior, Jesus Christ. During this special time of year, people of all faiths amicably come together to show expressions of love, charity, and appreciation towards others.

On June 27, 2016, at 6:50 am, I awakened with a fierce urgency to write. Whenever, this happens, I never know exactly what words will flow down from

Heaven. However, in obedience, I got up and grabbed my pen, a sheet of paper and wrote "A Christmas Gift." Most remarkable is that this poem was not written during the time of year that we actually celebrate Christmas. Instead, it came to me in the heat of the summer, when the holiday season was far from my mind. Yet, I was taken away in the spirit to the frostiness of a cold December night and actually envisioned staring out of the window at a deer bowing as it was left captivated by the magnificent nativity scene.

This poem encapsulates the enchanting beauty and wonder of the Christmas Season. The magical gift of witnessing an animal bowing in reverence to a nativity scene mesmerizes as an unforgettable and stark admonition: "Let everything that hath breath praise the Lord. Praise ye the Lord" (Psalms 150:6).

"LAUGH YOURSELF WHOLE"

Bench Note

I love to laugh at myself. I often think about the time that my mother asked me to bring her a bowl of ice cream and I did. The only problem was being stressed from studying for the bar exam, I put the ice cream in the kitchen cabinet instead of the freezer. The next morning, we both woke up to a very unpleasant surprise. At first, I asked myself, "How could you do something so dumb?" Then I laughed and laughed and laughed. In fact, I laughed so hard that I cried from laughter. Truth is, that was one of the best laughs I have ever had.

That boisterous laughter was an eye opener for me. It was then that I realized that my mistakes do not define me. So, my journey of laughing at my silly mistakes began. By laughing at myself, I was actually practicing the best method of self-correction. That ice cream fiasco happened many, many years ago, but I can assure you that I have never put ice cream in the kitchen cabinet again. Ironically, I have found that the more I laugh at my own mistakes, the more I grow.

There are some lessons in life that we are taught. However, the best lessons in life are actually "bought." The "bought lessons" are those that cause us to closely re-examine the motives of our actions and force us to look more closely within. With the "bought lessons," you remember where you made the wrong turn and vow to never make *that* mistake again. You can't forget those "bought" lessons. In fact, don't even try to forget them. Instead, just sit back and enjoy laughing at them with a giant bowl of ice cream.

"To everything there is a season, and a time to every purpose under the heaven: A time to weep, and a time to laugh; a time to mourn, and a time to dance."

Ecclesiastes 3:1, 4 (King James Version)

"LAUGH YOURSELF WHOLE"
Inspirational Dialogue

We all can use a good laugh. In fact, learning to laugh in difficult times is the measure of a cheerful heart and can often be the best medicine (Proverbs 17:22). Laughter is a great healer that forces us to release our cares and enjoy a humorous moment. Far too often, we are burdened and consumed with dark thoughts that seek to overtake our joy. However, when we take time to find the humor in everyday moments, we refuel our spirits. This allows us to let go and cope with life's many difficult challenges.

We all can recall something silly that we or our loved ones said or did that was worthy of laughter. It is good to recall such funny moments. This frees us to relax and release anxieties or stress. We should always make a conscious effort to take time to enjoy the humor in life. Let go and have fun! For, laughter and ice cream are miraculous gifts sent by God to heal the wounded spirit!

"BE STILL!"
Bench Note

There's a quiet awakening that happens when you unplug in life. Turning off cell phones, TVs, mobile devices, ear plugs, and video games can surround you with a peace serene, if you will simply let it in. Therein, is a calmness that seeks to overtake you and a joy that will overflow. In the quiet moments, you can reconnect with God to rediscover the true meaning and beauty of life. You can exhale to self-reflect and develop a deeper relationship with yourself. You finally put your own needs first and remove the noise that clutters the mind and clouds the ability to recognize that you can never achieve all that God created you to be until you first discover who you really are. So, how do you come to this place of perfect peace? It's quite simple: be still and then, just be still.

"Be still, and know that I am God: I will be exalted among the heathen, I will be exalted in the earth."

Psalms 46:10 (King James Version)

"BE STILL!"
Inspirational Dialogue

God always seeks a deeper and more meaningful relationship with His children. However, to achieve a complete union, we must first tune out the noise and clutter that prevents us from tuning into Him alone. Certainly, there are times that we are called into action. However, there are also moments in which we just need to sit down and be still. During these quiet times, we can peacefully listen with our heart to God's instructive messages and guidance.

We all need time alone to meditate, reflect, and seek direction regarding the paths that we have chosen. Often, we need redirection but just don't know what to do. Talking to others may provide some temporary assistance. However, only when you are still, rest in the Lord, and wait patiently for Him to act will you find perfect reassurance that only He can give (Psalms 37:7). Then, and only then, will the peace of God, which defies all human understanding, keep your heart and mind through Christ Jesus (Philippians 4:7).

"MESSAGE FROM THE MOON"

If the moon could speak from the heavens

What a story would be told

For it has witnessed great untold secrets

Before God's glories will unfold

The moon was there at man's creation

It saw from heaven when Satan fell

When Adam was sent from Eden

Not a whisper did it tell

The moon has seen all of man's transgressions

Wicked hearts encased in sin

Ruthless acts towards one another

Evil spirits lurking within

Yet, the moon still shines upon earth

Giving light for all to see

An ever presence set to guide

Pointing the way towards eternity

But, if the moon could speak unto us
Just a few words it would say
For its light burns like a candle and
It must be on its way

Oh, the words the moon would tell us
Could change the paths of all mankind
But only if we will listen
With our heart and not the mind

Its message is quite simple
With compassion all must live
Respecting those who transgress against you
Forgiveness, always freely give

By showing love for another
This will pass the tests of time
Though generations will fade before you
True love lingers for all mankind

Your smile can brighten darkness
Bringing lost souls into the light
Taking time to show others kindness
Can spur the blinded and give them sight

No good deed is gone unnoticed
Men take heed and follow suit
Be the change the world's awaiting
Let the difference start with you

Find common ground among your enemies
For you all bleed just the same
In the end all souls must journey
To the Creator from which it came

"The earth *is* the Lord's, and the fulnest thereof; the world, and they that dwell therein. For he hath founded it upon the seas, and established it upon the floods. Who shall ascend into the hill of the Lord? or who shall stand in his holy place? He that hath clean hands, and a pure heart; who hath not lifted up his soul unto vanity, nor sworn deceitfully. He shall receive the blessing from the Lord, and righteousness from the God of his salvation."

Psalms 24: 1-5 (King James Version)

"MESSAGE FROM THE MOON"
Inspirational Dialogue

When God created heaven and earth, he made two great lights: the greater light to rule the day (sun) and the lesser light to rule the night (moon). He also made the stars (Genesis 1:1, 16). It is riveting to gaze upon the sun and moon in amazement that, although created many years ago, they still exist to continuously shine beautiful light upon the earth.

On October 21, 2018, my husband and I were celebrating our 30th wedding anniversary in London, England and decided to take a day trip to visit Paris on the train. It was a wonderful day full of fun and celebration. It was late when we traveled back to London. The lights on the train were darkened for the passengers to sleep. As my husband peacefully slept at my side, I gazed out of the left train window and was captivated by the most beautiful full moon that I had ever seen. The light of the moon appeared white, iridescent, and so bright that it mesmerized me and I could not look away. The moon captured my attention with an urgent message to convey to my spirit. I immediately felt that familiar urge to write and found a pen and paper on the train and quickly wrote "MESSAGE FROM THE MOON."

As I wrote this poem, I was reminded of God's unwavering and eternal love for mankind. My mind was then carried away to unfortunate moments in time "witnessed" by the moon when Adam and Eve were created and then cast out of Eden, due to disobedience; Satan's banishment from Heaven, due to arrogance and jealousy of God; man's constant feuding and engagements in deadly wars; horrible pandemics; world famines; and persistent trouble throughout the beautiful land that God created.

Nevertheless, God has steadfastly declared in His word that "if my people, which are called by my name, shall humble themselves, and pray, and seek my face, and turn from their wicked ways; then will I hear from heaven, and will forgive their sin, and will heal their land" (2 Chronicles 7:14). "MESSAGE FROM THE MOON" is a potent reminder of the commandment that we love one another as Jesus has loved us (John 15:12). For, at the end of life's journey, every soul inevitably goes back to the Creator of the Universe from which it came.

"ALL BARK AND NO BITE!"
Bench Note

He would bark incessantly at that car. Every time our son got into his vehicle, our boxer dog would go absolutely crazy barking with rage. He would run back and forth, lunging towards the car and trying to reach his paws through the cast iron gate that separated them. After weeks of enduring this ridiculous display of aggression, I got fed up with standing idly by and decided to take a stand. What did I do? Instead of pulling out of the driveway to reach my destination, I backed up, got out of my car, opened the fence and literally "let the dog out."

So, what did our boxer do? As I expected, he ran right past our son's car, as if it didn't exist. I told him that this was his chance to "go get the car!" You know what he did? He looked at me with his head cocked sideways, as if I had two heads. Just as I suspected, our dog was literally "all bark and no bite." That ridiculous display of barking, with nothingness, reminded me that experiences we often dread and anticipate will shake us to our very core either never materialize, or have no meaningful impact. The real challenge in life is to overlook the "noise" and find the inner strength to boldly confront the unknown, realizing that most fears are often undeserved.

Today, our boxer still annoyingly barks at our cars, but I learned a valuable lesson that day. Whenever I really want to shut him up, instead of standing idly by and powerlessly listening to all of his noise, I just simply smile and open the gate.

"For God hath not given us a spirit of fear; but of power, and of love, and of a sound mind."

2 Timothy 1:7 (King James Version)

"ALL BARK AND NO BITE!"
Inspirational Dialogue

We all endure fears of the unknown at some point during out lifetime. We are often consumed with worry and can articulate something that contaminates our thoughts. Undoubtedly, we are convinced that some new challenge outweighs the last one that overtook us. However, can you even remember what you worried about on Thursday three weeks ago, last week, or even last year? Probably not, since most of us have already cast aside the old worries and chosen to replace them with newer worries. But, don't even bother thinking about the new worries for too long because soon, those worries will also be replaced.

Like our barking dog, this vicious cycle will continue until there is a conscious decision made to change that learned pattern of behavior. Clearly, the spirit of worry and fear is not given to us by God. In fact, Jesus explicitly tells us not to worry and take no thought about having enough food, drink, or clothing, since our Heavenly Father already knows that we have need of such things before we even ask him.

However, to receive these blessings, remove all doubts, fears of worry, and rise to our fullest potential, all required is that you seek first the kingdom of God and His righteousness and all these things shall be added unto you (Matthew 6:25-33). Just as I made the conscious decision to force our boxer dog to either "put up or shut up," we all are given a choice to either remain bound and accept our fears, or simply open the gate to freedom and walk into our divine destiny.

| Carol Walker-Russell, J.D. |

"YOUR MESS IS YOUR MESSAGE!"
Bench Note

Many of us are born into a messy life, while others just gravitate into one. Dysfunctional parents, infidelity, broken homes, death of loved ones, sickness, animus siblings, anonymous relatives, acrimonious neighbors, spiteful co-workers, unappreciative employers, and unexpected unemployment are just some of the messes in life that have no respect for any person. They can and often will happen to us all. When these messes happen, you may feel blindsided, helpless, and unable to cope with the difficult situation.

Often, there is the temptation to wallow in self-pity and seek comfort in either the wrong people or the wrong things. Therein, is the complete lack of understanding that messes come not to destroy you, but to strengthen your resolve and make you stronger. Ironically, each difficult situation actually chips away at the flaws in your character that keep you from embracing your true identity. Messes help to maximize your endowed inner-strength. While there are some messes in life that we don't get to choose, there are so many other messes that we bring on ourselves as a result of bad choices that we have purposefully made. Regardless, when faced with a mess you need to immediately seek a resolution. Complaining about the mess won't bring change. Wallowing in the mess won't help either. Instead, make a conscious and deliberate decision to move beyond the mess, so you can enter into your true purpose.

You will never grow your inner strength, or reach your full potential, by remaining stagnant in a messy life. Instead, choose wisely to remove the mess and watch your inner strength and character blossom. One day, after growing into such a mature understanding, you can look back with clarity and recognize that what once was your mess, has now become an ordained message.

"And we know that all things work together for good to them that love God, to them who are the called according to *his* purpose."

Romans 8:28 (King James Version)

"YOUR MESS IS YOUR MESSAGE!"
Inspirational Dialogue

God has promised salvation and a new life to those accepting Christ as his Son and the risen Savior (John 3:16). Even so, the lives of Christian believers are far from perfection, often chaotic, and definitely "messy." The bible clearly tells us: "Man that is born of a woman is of few days, and full of trouble (Job 14:1)." Therefore, we should not be surprised when life's unexpectancies arise and things feel out of control. Still, we are gifted with the Holy Spirit who was sent by God to teach, comfort, and guide us through each trial and tribulation (John 14:16-17).

Often, the problem is that we choose to ignore the guidance of the Holy Spirit and seek resolution on our own. This is a huge mistake! By accepting Christ, you have already received the anointing of the Holy Spirit, which abides within. You don't have to figure things out on your own or need anyone else to teach you what to do, or what is right. The Holy Spirit teaches you all things, is truth, and is no lie (1 John 2:27).

Therefore, lean first on the spirit of truth to guide you through trials and tribulations, trusting that he will show you what to do and lead you on the path to righteousness. Your life may be a complete "mess" right now, and that's okay because it is temporary. The good news is that all tribulations work together for good and with the right guidance, become a strong message of faith, hope, trust, and endurance.

"THE CONDEMNING BELT"

Bench Note

A little boy stood anxiously before his mother holding a thick brown belt in his hand. He was eager to share with her the details of all the wrongs that his little brother had done throughout the day while she was at work.

He smiled with a crooked grimace as he parlayed each transgression of his small younger brother in detail. When he finished, he looked up into the loving eyes of his mother, handed her the belt, and asked her this question: "Now Mama, what are you going to do about it?"

Without missing a beat, his mother looked into her son's condemning eyes. Speaking softly and gently she replied: "Son, before we can talk about all of your brother's faults, first tell me about yours."

The little boy hung his head in shame and walked slowly away as tears rolled down his face. He knew that for all the wrongs he had done: the lies, trickery, stealing, fighting, bearing false witness, jealousy, judgment and condemnation of others, that thick brown belt he held in his hand was simply too small.

| Carol Walker-Russell, J.D. |

"Judge not, that ye be not judged. For with what judgment ye judge, ye shall be judged: and with what measure ye mete, it shall be measured to you again. And why beholdest thou the mote that is in thy brother's eye, but considerest not the beam that is in thine own eye?"

Matthew 7:1-3 (King James Version)

"THE CONDEMNING BELT"
Inspirational Dialogue

"The Condemning Belt" admonishes us not to judge others. We have all been guilty of critiquing and criticizing others at some point, especially our close family members. While it is easy to find fault and weaknesses in others, we often fail to use the same microscope to closely examine our own weaknesses and shortcomings. It is interesting that the little boy in "The Condemning Belt" was not only eager to tattle to his mother about the wrong doings of his younger brother, but actually held a belt in hand as he grimaced with a wicked spirit of eagerness to do so. It is most unfortunate when those closest to you not only know your deepest secrets, but are often the first people standing in the line of betrayal.

However, contrast the response of the little boy's mother, which represents the loving, kind, and gentle corrective spirit of God. In the end, the little boy realized that his sins far outweighed his brother's and his punishment would also be much greater.

The moral of this simple, yet compelling story is that no one should ever revel in finding and condemning the faults of others, without first considering their own. For, whatever judgment you give others, by that same measure will you also be judged. Simply put: "Judge not, and ye shall not be judged: condemn not, and ye shall not be condemned: forgive, and ye shall be forgiven" (Luke 6:37).

"HEALING RAIN"
Bench Note

There is healing in the cleansing of rain. Lightning flashes as the sky darkens, sending a warning of what is ahead. The sound of wind grows as the trees bend to salute the coming of the storm. Birds flee for safety to honor the magnitude of the moment. The rain slowly begins until its fierceness blows sideways. Cascading water flows with thunderous sounds, commanding reverence and respect. The loudness of the storm frightens yet leaves a calmness that touches the soul. The spirit awakens to the voice of a power far greater than its own. For a moment in time, the unification with God is met and sealed. There is healing power in the sound of rain. It calms the spirit and anchors the soul.

"That ye may be the children of your Father which is in heaven: for he maketh his sun to rise on the evil and on the good, and sendeth the rain on the just and on the unjust."

Matthew 5:45 (King James Version)

"HEALING RAIN"
Inspirational Dialogue

The storms of life are destined to fall on us all. Although we revel in the beautiful sunny days, rain is also necessary for our continued growth and development. God commands the rain to replenish the earth for the evolution of life and bring forth bountiful harvests of food for our consumption. Similarly, the most difficult "rainstorms of life" replenishes our soul, help us evolve, and draw us closer to God.

Some storms in life begin quietly and give little or no warning, such as a negative medical diagnosis found only through a routine physical examination; the sudden death of a loved one; or an unexpected job loss. Without the intervention of a loving God, these rainstorms would quickly shatter our world and lead us into blinding chaos. Yes, God sends rainstorms to fall on the just and the unjust. However, we are never left alone to weather the storms of life. For, we find comfort in knowing that "God is our refuge and strength, a very present help in trouble" (Psalms 46:1).

"MASTERPIECE!"
Bench Note

A woman had a fervent conversation with God. Father, she said, the people that you have placed among me are unkind. The gifts that I have given them remain unopened. The flowers that I give are cast aside. The kindness that I offer is rejected. All that I get in return are the crumbs that are cast from their tables. God, seeing her tears, gently wiped them away and replied: "Daughter, from those crumbs you have fed the hungry and clothed the naked. You have shown great love, despite receiving none in return and displayed mercy to the merciless. From those crumbs gathered, you have formed my greatest creation. For, you have become my Masterpiece!"

"But I say unto you which hear, Love your enemies, do good to them which hate you, Bless them that curse you, and pray for them which despitefully use you…And as ye would that men should do to you, do ye also to them likewise…But love ye your enemies, and do good, and lend, hoping for nothing again; and your reward shall be great, and ye shall be the children of the Highest: for he is kind unto the unthankful and to the evil."

Luke 6:27-28, 31, 35 (King James Version)

"MASTERPIECE!"
Inspirational Dialogue

The true testament of God's love is expressed by humbling ourselves through obedience in showing forgiveness and genuine kindness towards those who transgress against us. We are often jarred by the hurtful rejection or betrayal of others and find it most difficult to move beyond such painful disappointments. However, when we show mercy towards those who really don't deserve it, God will likewise show such mercy towards us. It is easy to only love those who do good things for us. We receive no reward for that. The true challenge is loving enemies who despise you, especially when they have been given no good cause.

Although it is perplexing to encounter people who hate you, showing such love towards them is not only expected from God, but required. Never choose to recompense to any person evil for evil (Romans 12:17). For, unreciprocated love shown towards your enemies does not go unnoticed by God, who sees your pain and renews your strength. You will not only be greatly rewarded because of obedience in loving your enemies and doing good toward those who hate you but become God's greatest "Masterpiece!"

"STRONGER THAN YOU THINK!"

When you think you've reached

Your breaking point

Heart burdened down with sin

God quickly sends His angels down

To lift you from within

There is nothing that you can do

To separate from His love

For it was founded upon the heavens and

Cast down from above

Your strength may weaken in trialed times

All hope, you fear is gone

But God will never leave you

For He is always strong

His power overcomes all fear

To cover you with His care

All thoughts of weakness disappears

When you go to God in prayer

God gently cradles you in His arms and
Wipes away all tears
Then casts away all thoughts of doubt
From hopelessness and fears

You're stronger than you think you are
With peace sent from above
Your faith and strength will be renewed
With God's eternal love

"I can do all things through Christ which strengtheneth me."
Philippians 4:13 (King James Version)

"STRONGER THAN YOU THINK!"
Inspirational Dialogue

Finding strength in times of weakness is one of the greatest challenges of our faith and trust in God. This is particularly true today as our nation and the world struggles with the COVID-19 pandemic. Many people have suffered greatly during this pandemic, which has caused debilitating sicknesses; sudden and unexpected deaths of loved ones; loss of businesses and jobs; evictions from home; food inadequacies; closures of schools; overwhelming panic; fear of the unknown; and feelings of despair and hopelessness due to the pandemic having no end in sight. Nevertheless, we are still not without hope when we continue to seek spiritual help as we trust and seek guidance from the Lord.

Instead of being anxious and dwelling on the fears of the unknown, take your cares and concerns to the Lord in prayer with acknowledgment and thanksgiving for what He has already done for you. It is amazing how fears are greatly diminished in prayers of praising and thanking God for His goodness and blessings throughout our lives. Finding peace in the middle of a storm is not only possible but guaranteed because God keeps those whose mind is stayed on Him with trust in perfect peace (Isaiah 26:3). Then, the peace of God, which surpasses all understanding will guard your heart and your mind through Christ Jesus (Philippians 4:6-7).

Even in the most difficult times, you are lovingly covered by God and stronger than you think when you do not rely on your own strength. Instead, keep your trust in the Lord with all of your heart and do not lean on your own understanding. In all your ways acknowledge him, and He shall direct your paths (Proverbs 3:5-6).

Biblical References, King James Version

LIVE A LASTING LEGACY!

"Finally, brethren, whatsoever things are true, whatsoever things are honest, whatsoever things are just, whatsoever things are pure, whatsoever things are lovely, whatsoever things are of good report; if there be any virtue, and if there be any praise, think on these things."

Philippians 4:8

May God's joy, peace, and grace be with you today and always!

Love and blessings,

Carol Walker-Russell, J.D.

Strolling in the Park,
Gatlinburg, Tennessee

Fishing in Hawaii with Greg

Touring Mount Kilauea

Anniversary
dinner with Greg
(Atlanta, Georgia)

Made in the USA
Columbia, SC
16 October 2020